Creation Speaks

Glenn Hass

Illustrations and Cover Design by Cindy Woolford

Winston-Derek Publishers, Inc.
Pennywell Drive—P.O. Box 90883
Nashville, TN 37209

© 1991 by Winston-Derek Publishers, Inc.

All rights reserved. No part of this book may be reproduced in any form without written permission from the publishers, except by a reviewer who may quote brief passages in a review to be printed in a newspaper or magazine.

First printing 1991
Second printing 1992
Third printing 1993

PUBLISHED BY WINSTON-DEREK PUBLISHERS, INC.
Nashville, Tennessee 37205

Library of Congress Catalog Card No: 89-52223
ISBN: 1-55523-322-8

Printed in the United States of America

This book is dedicated to
God, who inspired me;
my sisters, who stood by me;
my friends, who believed in me;
and to you,
a lovely part of God's creation.

Contents

The Letter 1
Creation Speaks 2
A Seed 3
Spring 4
Naked 5
Castles 6
Beaten 7
To Grass Lovers 8
Curious Kittens 9
Discovery 10
Puffs 11
How to Eat a Cloud 12
Stormy Feelings 13
Spring Beauty 14
Awake 15
Meeting 16
On the Street 17
Rat Race 18
Tension 19
Who Needs 'Em? 20
Black Marks 21
Who Me? 22
Why Mommy Why? 23
The Solution 24
Progress 25

Twelve Billion	26
Creation	27
One Small Heart	29
The Key	30
Why Did You Die?	31
Popcorn Popper	32
Dante De Lion	33
The Search	34
Little Boy Blue	35
I Saw	36
Squirrely	37
The Old Oak	38
The Pound	39
Ice Water	40
Love	41
Autumn Kiss	42
Please	43
Fish	44
Mosquito	45
Dreaming Trees	46
Quiet Glory	47
Winter Scenes	48
The Fly	49
Munching	50

The Letter

God sent me a letter
A long time ago,
Telling me
How things should be.
How to make this place
A liveable place,
A loveable space
For us.

To love the land
And till the earth.
To take command
And give it birth.

To be fruitful
And multiply.
To know his will,
And to keep it nigh.

CREATION SPEAKS

Red veined petals
Of royal hue
Delicate strength
Old
Yet ever new

The heavens rendered
Kiss the earth
Glory descending
Dying
And new birth

Stars forever
shine the light
Infinite darkness
Cut
By glory bright

In Flower's Growing
In Sun's Setting
In Heavens Flowing

Yes

Creation Speaks

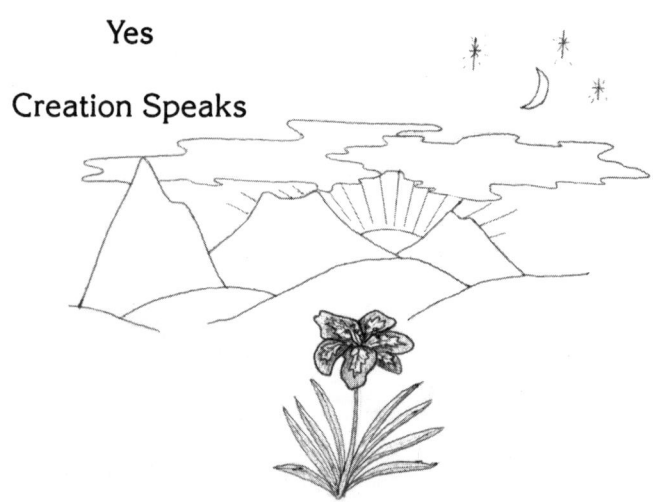

A Seed

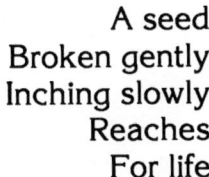

A seed
Touching tenderly
Barely broken earth
Trembles
With life

A seed
Broken gently
Inching slowly
Reaches
For life

A seed
Tasting sunlight
Reaching moisture
Deepens
Its life

A seed
In flowers fading
In winters coming
Begins again
Its life

Spring

Awake my soul
Rise with the flowers
Kiss the dew
Soak up the sun
Grow again

Naked

Listen to the
Weeping trees,
Sighing in the wind.
Gaze upon
Their silent tears,
Gold and crimson sin.

Castles

Simple castles
In the sand

Secret places
Lost from sight

Glowing embers
Light the day

Rising beauty
Touch the sky

Beaten

I've fought the best
And held my own,
Until you came
And chased me home.
    Little friend
    You've beaten me.
With balls of ice
And waves of snow,
Biting my face
And making me know
    you've beaten me.
I tried to fight,
Throwing snow at you,
But every time
It'd land on me too,
    until I knew you'd beaten me.
        Little cloud,
        you've beaten me.

To Grass Lovers

Why do you love grass?
Parched
Same
Brown grass.
Never changing,
Never ending,
Wounded
Tattered
Grass.
Never growing,
Never showing
What was meant to be.

Curious Kittens

Young Lions stalk the day,
Day we take for granted.
Young Lions take the way,
Way pawing with delight.

Every step a new adventure.
Every tail a circle chase.
Every string a web enchanted.
Every shoe a holy place.

Young Lions bless the soul,
Soul of those caught watching.
Young Lions make us whole,
Whole to be young with them.

Every stone a desert island.
Every moth a stately prize.
Every leaf a new invention.
Every turn a great surprise.

Discovery

One granule,
Two granules,
Three granules,
Four,
A million grains,
And I'm just one more.
Rolled out with the tide,
Brought in by the same.
With so many others,
I play the game.
One granule,
Two granules,
Three granules,
Four,
What am I
Rolling for?

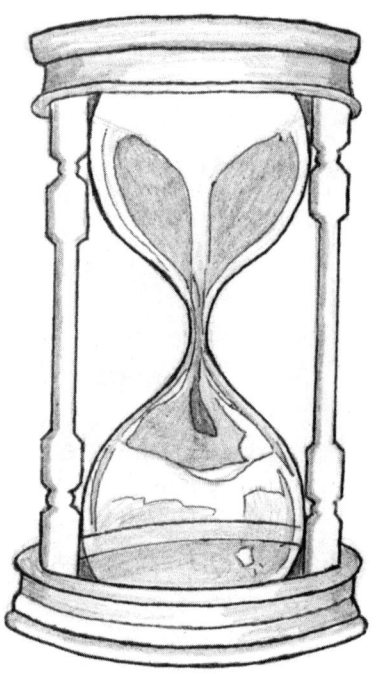

Puffs

Dandy
Dandy
Dandelions

Whirling winds of wonder
Whispers of delight
Tickling my cheek
Dancing out of sight

Dandy
Dandy
Dandelion Puffs

How to Eat a Cloud

It's not very hard,
Not as hard as it seems,
To munch on a cloud
And let yourself dream.

Just pick out a cloud.
Yes, pick out the best.
Then open your heart,
The soul does the rest.

Lifting and soaring,
Tumbling in snow,
Tasting sunlight,
Letting it flow,
Cotton Candy,
Popcorn,
Floating yummy white,
Oh, how good it tastes,
Each and every bite.

It's not very hard,
Not as hard as it seems,
To munch on a cloud
And let yourself dream.

Stormy Feelings

The flash of lightning
Breathes life into the sky.
Seeing moments
Clear, before they die.

Deafening silence
After the thunder crack.
Emptiness filled
And then given back.

Wet curtains are drawn,
Cascading past my face.
Stormy feelings
In a quiet place.

Spring Beauty

Capture
The flavor
The sight
The touch
Of spring
Delicate petals
Budding life
Flowing streams
Pink delight
Small
Lovely
Many
Signs of spring

AWAKE

Ugly oyster
Open wide
Finds the treasure
Deep inside

Sleeping cocoon's
Final break
Shows the beauty
Now awake

Fighting infant's
Virgin cry
Touch the glory
Breathe the sigh

Meeting

Fiery carpet
Quench my thirst
Draw me ever
Nearer earth
Meeting at horizon's point
Kissing now
The heavens reddened
Join

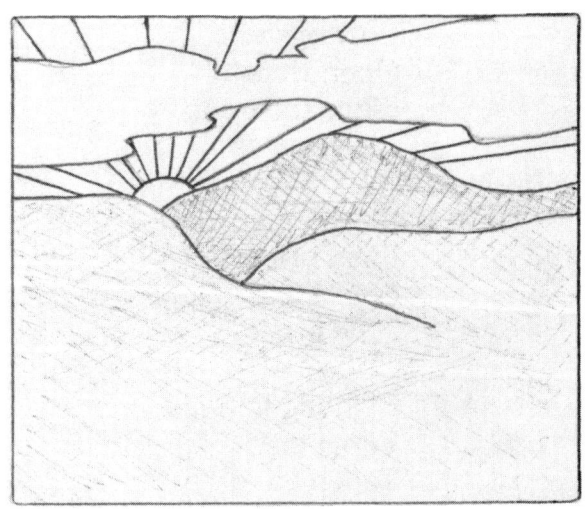

On the Street

Why did they die,
The little ones,
New life passing?

Did they forget
To look both ways
Before crossing?

Going too slow
Moving too fast,
Slain for being?

Did a loved one
See it happen,
Life blood flowing?

Did the driver
Even notice,
Tires bumping?

RAT RACE

There they go!
The racing rats,
Past the turnstile
And down the isle,
Grabbing what they can.

What a show
On flying feet.
Looking for ways,
Caught in the maze,
Searching for the cheese.

Watch them slow
Through winding ways.
Lost in long halls,
Finding blank walls,
Losing a slim chance.

Now they know
The fearful fate.
Chasing their tails,
Learning to fail,
Dying in the cage.

TENSION

The heaven pulls the sun,
    The sun pulls the earth,
        The earth pulls the moon,
    The moon pulls the tide,
The tide pulls our lives,
    We live in the web.

WHO NEEDS 'EM?

Alligators, Crocodiles,
Who needs 'em?
Elephants in the wild,
Who needs 'em?
Sea Lions and Otters too,
Who needs 'em?
And all the bird do do,
Who needs 'em?
Wild woods and sticky swamps,
Who needs 'em?
Little kids making camp,
Who needs 'em?
Killer Whales and Porpoises,
Who needs 'em?

. . . Ain't I enough to fill this place?

Black Marks

His fault,
Her fault,
Never mine.
Me?
I'm just
Marking time.

What I do,
What I say,
Never mine.
Me?
I'm just
Marking time.

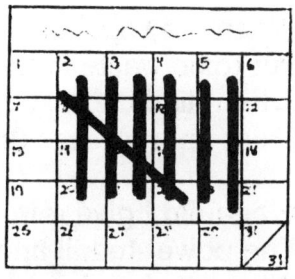

Birds die,
Fish die,
Never mind.
Me?
I'm just
Marking time.

What's not done,
What's not said,
Never mine.
Me?
I'm just
Marking time.

WHO ME?

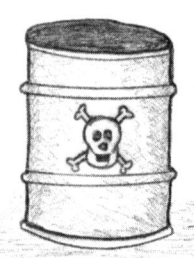

When did I spill oil,
Put toxic waste in the soil?
When did I choke the air,
Treat animals less than fair?

When did I give rain,
The power to kill and maim?
When did I make this place,
Unfit for the human race?

When I did not fight,
Though my heart knew what was right.
I gave away my choice,
When I did not lift my voice.

Why Mommy Why?

Why Mommy why?
Why can't I
Stand in the rain
And watch it stain
My dress?

Why Mommy why?
Why can't I
Go out and play,
Beautiful day
All red?

Why Mommy why?
Why do people die?

THE SOLUTION   (Tune: "Bringing in the Sheaves")

Rainin' gasoline,
Rainin' gasoline,
Maybe it'd solve our problems,
Rainin' gasoline.

Energy's a problem,
Gets bigger every day.
We've got the solution,
That works in every way.

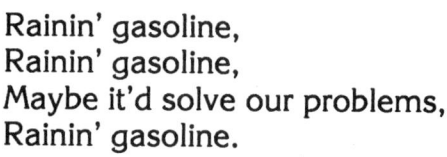

Rainin' gasoline,
Rainin' gasoline,
Maybe it'd solve our problems,
Rainin' gasoline.

We dump it in the oceans,
A billion gallons a day.
And soon we'll be a croakin',
A billion souls a day.

Rainin' gasoline,
Rainin' gasoline,
Maybe it'd solve our problems,
Rainin' gasoline.

From Aardvark to Amoeba,
All will be washed away.
Nothin' left but petrol,
Forever and a day.

Rainin' gasoline,
Rainin' gasoline,
Yes it would solve our problems,
Rainin' gasoline.

In memory of the Arctic and Antarctic oil spills 1988-89

Progress

They call it
Progress
Progress
Boldness and Blunder
Often we wonder
Whatever will be

They call it
Progress
Progress
Blindness and Building
So often killing
What we can't see

They call it
Progress
Progress
Death and Destruction
Born of corruption
We pay the fee

They call it
Progress
Progress
Blind and Believing
Never perceiving
We are the key.

TWELVE BILLION

Twelve billion mouths
How do we feed them
Twelve billion mouths
How do we heed them

Twelve billion wars
How do we fight them
Twelve billion wars
How do we right them

Twelve billion homes
How do we make them
Twelve billion homes
Where do we take them

Twelve billion flushes
Where will it go now
Twelve billion flushes
Where will it flow now

Twelve billion souls
We can't support them
Twelve billion souls
We can't deport them

Twelve billion

CREATION

Children born upon the
plains,
And my heart was glad.
You took the fields,
And I was not sad.

Fallen timber built your
homes
On every hilltop.
Warm by your fires,
You could see no stop.

Cities built on river's edge
Gave me human waste.
You took no heed
In your human haste.

Bigger better every year,
Double what you give.
Rivers choked now,
Fish, they cannot live.

Steam roller of destruction,
To see was to take.
You took it all,
Took for taking's sake.

I tried to clean up your mess,
Rinsed it from the sky.
But you sent more,
Made the rivers die.

The oceans have become filled
With the stink of death.
Count your days now,
Humans have no health.

Children die upon the plains,
My heart is not there.
I gave it all,
But you took no care.

ONE SMALL HEART

Waves stand up
Waters part
Heaven forming
One small heart

Trees bow down
Flowers cry
Children growing
Touch the sky

Clouds will weep
Shadows call
Branches bending
Start to fall

Hills call out
Valleys pray
Heaven ending
One small day

The Key

From the dark,
Man
Lit a fire
Warmed his heart
Built it higher

From the cold
Man
Built warm walls.
Made his home
In family halls.

From hunger,
Man
Tilled the earth.
Made the food
To feed his birth.

From his thirst,
Man
Found a source.
Dug a well
And changed its course.

From today,
Man
Is the key.
That will change
The world we see.

Why Did You Die?

Mother,
Why did you die?
Won't you awake,
Comfort my cry?

Warm gentle fur,
Long caring ears,
Cold tickling nose,
Killer of fears . . .

Mother,
Why did you die?
I saw your blood,
I heard it cry.

Why did you die?

Stomping of feet,
Thunder of guns,
Baying of hounds,
Who has won?

Why mother,
Why did you die?

For you,
My little rabbit,
For you.
What else could I do?
The guns were after you.

POPCORN POPPER

Popcorn popper in the sky,
Pop your corn and let it fly.
Floating here,
Floating there,
Strung by threads of silent air,
Following the gentle breeze,
Falling slowly through the trees,
Till resting in the bowls of earth,
They become balls of mirth.
Popcorn popper in the sky,
Pop your corn and let it fly.

DANTE DE LION

Dandelion feathers
Floating in the wind.
Bringing winter's joy
Blooming into spring.

THE SEARCH

Weed of seed
Searching for light,
Killing others
Knowing you're right.
Climbing hills and valleys,
Climbing dales and lanes,
Searching for freedom,
Searching in vain.

Bound by water
Bound by light
Bound by earth
Try as you might

Weed of seed
Can't you see,
Only with others
Will you be free.

LITTLE BOY BLUE

Silent sleeping,
Little boy blue.
Huddled and bunched
In winter attire.
Rocked to sleep
On bumpy bus tires.
Warm eyes,
Happy smiles,
He awakens
After miles.

I Saw

Horse's head,
Alligator's teeth,
Flying dragons,
Gray underneath;
Ten tons or more
I know you weigh,
And yet you soar,
Darkening the day.

Squirrelly

Nuts!
Where . . .
Under the tree?
Did . . .
Next to the hole?
I . . .
Under the leaf?
Put . . .
Next to the pole?
Those . . .
What could this be?
Nuts . . .
My mouth is full!
Oops . . .
Nuts!

The Old Oak

Wise old oak,
Why do you cling
To faded memories?
    of springing buds
    of warming earth
    of amber leaves
Don't you know
Spring has come?
And you can't grow
Because of memories.

THE POUND

Alone
In a cage
Together
They wait
For
Death
Empty Eyes
Searching
For a hope
Any chance
To live

Ice Water

Warm currents of spring
Melt the driven snow
Clear mountain brook
Pure crystal flow

Soft covers of mist
Hide the coming light
Brief treasure lent
Dark floating night

Cool curtains of rain
Soak the thawing field
Small bursting seeds
Sweet mountain yield

LOVE

Little blossom
Picked with care
Why do you wilt
Dying here
In my loving hands?

Autumn Kiss

Autumn breeze
Brush the sky

Amber waves
Now set free

Naked trees
Stop to smile

Fallen days
Kiss the night

Please

Many,
Many,
Raindrops
Knocking on my door.
Many,
Many,
Raindrops
Dripping on my floor.
Making puddles
For my ducks.
Making rivers
For my trucks.
Mommy,
Mommy,
Couldn't I
Please let this water lie?

FISH

If I were a fish,
What fish would I be?
I'd be a little fish,
That no one could see.

    I'd never be eaten,
    I'd never be beaten,
    By any other fish.

    I'd never be sought,
    And never be caught,
    So this is what I wish,

To be a little fish,
That no one can see.

Mosquito

Humming now
At twenty feet
Espying out
Some human meat
I sight some
Unshod feet
Oh
What a delightful treat
Diving
Now
Faster
Than
A
Hand
I Attack
This unaware man
The bite is bitten
The blood is gotten
And I'll
Not soon
Be forgotten.

Dreaming Trees

Age of passion
Shorter day
Longer night
Ebbing of the tide
Burst of fading light

Coat of color
Golden mist
Amber hue
Beauty of the wind
Catch of autumn dew

Sleep of wonder
Barren branch
Fallen leaves
Blanket of the hill
Dawn of dreaming trees

Quiet Glory

Scarlet leaves,
Dance for me.
Holy fire,
Light the tree.

Autumn breeze,
Brush the sky.
Scared beauty,
Slowly die.

Amber waves,
Touch the throne.
Golden ocean,
Gentle home.

Fallen days,
Kiss the night.
Quiet glory,
Tender sight.

Winter Scenes

Here they come
The light-n-crusty
Slightly dusty,
Cold-n-mighty
Snow sands.

Warm white blanket
On a cool north wind
Cover me up
As winter descends

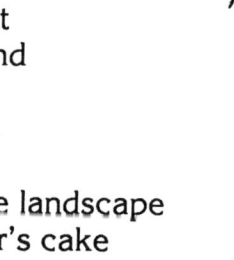

Gentle covers of the landscape
Frosting on a winter's cake
Leaves upon the barren trees now
Joys of winter I partake.

THE FLY

Buzzing through the midnight air,
Flew the fly without a care.
Buzzing loudly,
So all could hear.
Buzzing loudly,
So all would fear.
His oh so dreadful bite.

He saw a subject
Far below,
Bowing so gracelessly.

Buzzing at this maddening sight,
He flew right down
To give a bite.

To meet him came a welcome rug.
That gave him such a dreadful hug,
And drew him in an open mouth.
Burp
Rib-it
What a tasty bug.

Munching

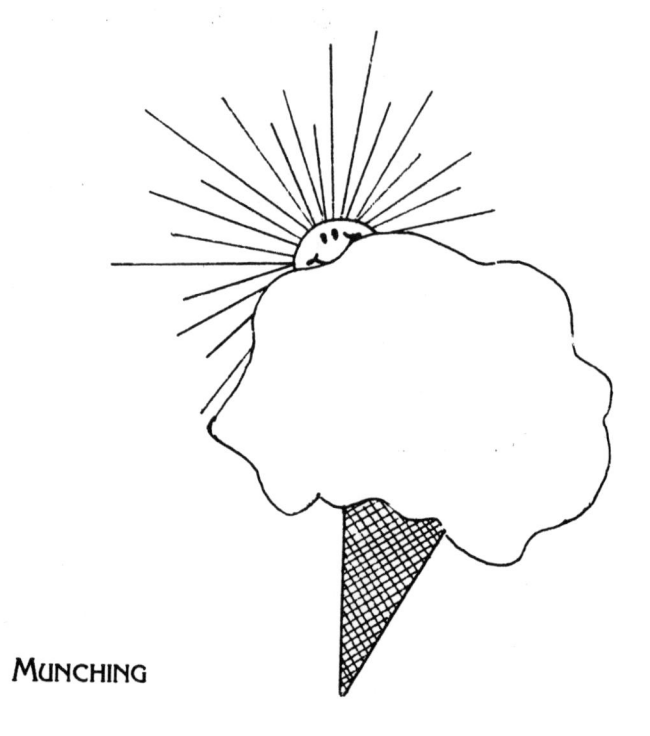

Today is a cloud munching day
Mouth watering
Tingling
Tasty
Cloud munching day.